love,

the one that got away

shana schoone

for the ones that got away

letters

introduction   02

the one that gave me everything
but everything was a lie   07

the one that self-sabotaged   53

the one that went ghost   93

the one that moved away   129

the one that let me go   143

no one in particular   161

"the one"   181

anyone reading this   195

my love,

by the time you see this, these words may no longer resonate for me but perhaps they will for you or a part of you that still remains.

you may think you know the men in this book, but i can guarantee you, you don't. i knew most of them for years. i saw different versions of them over time. they were my friends, most of them lovers. some i even painted with my own trauma, i'll admit. others didn't have a good bone in their body, so i added one. lately, i've been consumed with thoughts of duality. drowning in the idea that we are both a villain in one person's story and a hero in another's. no one is innocent in these pages, not even me. no matter how badly i wanted to be. i think love makes us do crazy things in an attempt to escape the pain it could cause. however, i've learned that it's not love that causes the pain. instead, it's the crazy things.

i say i loved each one of these men. but to tell you the absolute truth, i'm not sure i know what romantic love truly is. maybe i've felt it too much or not at all. to me, love will always be liberating. i think that's both the rose and the thorn to knowing me and loving me. at the end of the day, i could love you for all you are just to leave you or let you leave me. i've always chosen freedom over any man. even a man who only wants me to be free. sometimes, i even think that loving me is intimidating. i give you a safe place to share things with me you've never told anyone. hard truths you didn't know you harbored until they were spoken into existence right in front of me. i see through you. that can make anyone run away while simultaneously making me fall into something i'd call love. the only issue arises when it's hard for me to feel safe enough with men to not only open up but stay after doing so.

everything expressed on these pages is true according to some version of myself that needed to be heard. these are the love letters to five men that i will never send. maybe because i find my words too late or i tell myself they wouldn't care. i'm rarely vulnerable until it's time to move on, and the only way for me to do that is to write. in a way, this is a funeral for past love. however, at funerals we pick up more love than we came with. the funny thing about grief is we wouldn't have it without love. endings seem to remind us that nothing else matters. i'd like to argue that love is the only thing that lasts even when a connection dies. i hope you find everything you need in these pages. may you find the anger and betrayal you forgot about. may you remember why you had to meet them. most of all, may you let the love last because that's the only door to peace and moving on.

i love you,
shana schoone

the one that
gave me everything
but everything
was a lie,

i rambled on about my life,
and you just listened
until you asked, "can i stop you for a second?"
"of course," i said.
"i've realized i'm obsessed with you."
six words that would be the end
of anything with anyone else,
but from you they felt like the beginning,
they felt like everything my life had been missing.

i didn't know how to say
those three little words then,
but the way you looked at me,
i knew i had to say something.
so, i grabbed your hand,
looked in your eyes,
and said,
"i want you to know
you have the power to ruin my life,
so, if one day you decide to leave me
just let me down easy–
i'm sensitive
and you'd be the greatest heartbreak
of my entire life.
sure, i'd write a killer book off of it in the end
and make millions,
but i'd rather have you by my side".

loving you
was like standing in the pouring rain–
i was liberated,
i was a mess,
but i kinda liked it.
i wasn't worried about the aftermath;
all i could do was enjoy the dance.
i didn't want an umbrella;
i liked to feel the rain on my skin.
i didn't want to protect myself
from getting wet;
i wanted to be drenched–
i wanted to be consumed by it.

i like the feeling of meeting your person
in the beginning,
where you realize you'll never have these moments
or feelings again
because each one
is a memory,
a movie.
i like slowly watching their 'tonight's'
turn into 'tn's' just like mine
and the silences,
say i **love** you for the first time.
i hate the awkwardness,
but i like knowing it's the last i'll experience.
i like how it's hard to say goodbye,
i like being able to look into someone's eyes
and see forever.

i was lying in this bed
three nights ago,
coming down from the high
that is your love,
thanking God and all my lucky stars
for the amazing person you are.

and tonight
i'm wondering where you've gone.

you wouldn't let me cook for you
or take care of you when you were sick,
and if i had been a woman who wasn't in **love**,
i would have known then.
i wouldn't have had to wait to read the words
"i think this is the end"
from a text
that disrespected
all the time we had spent.

did you know
that was our last moment together?
did you plan it?
when you hugged me one final time,
did you get to feel it?
because i didn't–
i didn't know.

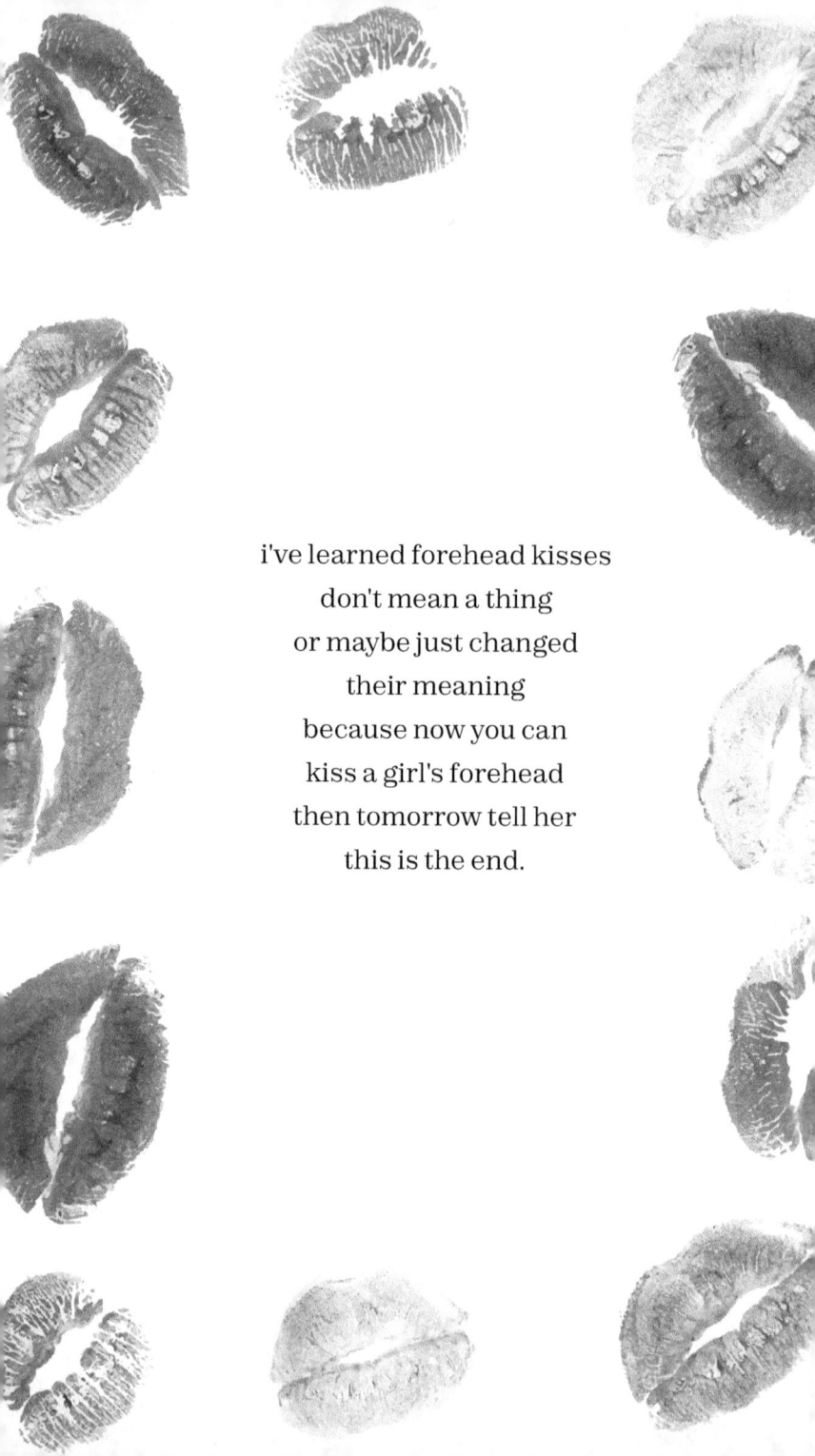

i've learned forehead kisses
don't mean a thing
or maybe just changed
their meaning
because now you can
kiss a girl's forehead
then tomorrow tell her
this is the end.

maybe if i never open your last message,
it'll never be over.
and i'll wake up every morning to you
like nothing's changed.
happy and excited,
i'll spend the day
thinking about a future with you–
texting you random things–
and i'll never know the feeling
of waking up and not being able to breathe.

i left a toothbrush at your house;
there wasn't a sign not to.

i left a toothbrush at your house
believing i'd use it again.

i left a toothbrush at your house
thinking we were making progress.

i left a toothbrush at your house
fantasizing about the day
all my things would be there.

i left a toothbrush at your house
because that day you told me you **loved** me.

i left a toothbrush at your house,
but i forgot to tell you.

i left a toothbrush at your house,
and i don't want it back.

i left a toothbrush at your house.

tell me, when you saw it,
did you throw it away?

or because it was the last thing
you had left from me,

did you let it stay?

it's been two weeks
since we separated
and i still call you my boyfriend
to those who ask.
i don't know why,
in the moment it just feels right,
and i smile because it makes me
think of when you were mine.
for a second
i don't have to think
about the past two weeks.
it just feels nice.

when you're heart broken
everything becomes a task:
waking up,
going to bed,
brushing your hair–
each day feels like an eternity.
but as you watch time
slip through the cracks
suddenly,
you're getting farther and farther
from the happiest days of your life.

you were a first date and a surprising second, followed by a third and a fourth. and sometime after the sixth you slowly, or maybe too quickly, became a part of my life. suddenly, we had a history and a future. there was a time i thought we would never be nothing.

i'm so upset with you,
but if i was in the same room as you,
i know i couldn't help but smile–
and that upsets me even more.

i refuse to believe we aren't meant to be,
maybe not in the future
not days, weeks, months, or even years from now,
but you and i
we were meant to be,
we were meant to meet
at the exact time we did,
in the exact place we did.
we were meant to have that time together–
we were meant for target runs, spontaneous
adventures, favorite movies, and laughter;
we were meant for slow kisses, nice dinners,
playing we aren't really strangers, and watching
endless episodes of how i met your mother.
you're not the one that i'll marry
or even someone i'll speak with again,
but you were the one for me
at that time in my life,
and we were meant to be
even if it wasn't for forever.

but we don't
have memories.
all we have
are lies.

there are things that hurt worse
than losing someone who cared about you,
and that's learning
that they never did.

i'm not a very proper woman,
and i don't aim to be.
i think proper
is just another name for property.
i think proper belongs to those
who die a little too early
or sell their soul for a lamborghini.
yes, i'll cross my legs but not because
you tell me to act like a lady,
and i'll always choose my own authenticity
over your desire of having me in slavery.
and i like when you shake your head at me—
it lets me know i'm not just another copy,
i'm not someone you're going to meet again,
and you'll be haunted by my memory
because i'm someone you won't be able to forget.
i'm not someone who can't think for a living,
i don't need your approval or your pity
and that's why i **love** unconditionally.
and loving me was your first taste of liberty
and if i'm not the woman you want to marry,
this is the last time you'll see me.

i wish money could buy me–
i wish our dream house you just bought
to win me back
could make me forget
about everything else i want.
i wish money could fill every void
i'd have without my self-expression.
i wish money and you
could be all i'd ever need,
i wish i'd let you control me,
i wish you weren't so stubborn like me–
my life could be so easy.
i wish money could buy me,
and it'd be enough for me
just to have your **love**
and warm body beside me.

unless your
currency is love,
my love cannot
be bought.

you love my beauty–
it's what brought you to me,
but you hate how others like it too.
you hate the idea of them taking me from you,
so maybe today
you take me off social media,
and i don't get any self-expression,
but i can have everything i want
or everything you think i want,
and tomorrow maybe i'll be happy–
dripped in louis or fendi–
then maybe after that,
i'll be lonely,
not because the world isn't watching me,
but because i never catch you listening.

your heart's ugly,
so you wear lies like makeup.

if they can lie about eating the last piece of
chocolate cake, they can lie about anything.

i know more than you think i do;
i know enough to know i've been lied to.

it was never **love**

because you never **loved** yourself.

in one month

you were my man,

carli's man,

courtney's man,

and ria's man–

but you never were yourself.

i haven't said anything.
but i know.
you know.
i know.

never trust someone
who doesn't like water–
they don't like what's good for them.

maybe it was my fault.
i wanted you to be someone else;
i wanted to look in your eyes
and see more than dollar signs.
i wanted to look in your eyes
and not see lies.
i wanted to look in your eyes
and feel something,
anything,
just one time.

i was a chess piece
in your game,
you were a player
using me
until the game was over,
or until you got bored,
i never understood chess anyway.

i'm not angry with you,
i'm past that.
i'm not going to yell at you,
i'm past that too.
i don't even have an argument for you.
in fact,
i have nothing left,
nothing left but silence–
a silence that will take away
the only thing you ever wanted from me
in the first place:
my attention.
and for that reason,
my silence will cut you like a knife.

it hurts when you don't get attention,
doesn't it?
perhaps it reminds you of when you didn't get it
from your parents,
and you needed it–
you still do.
after all,
that's why you lie
to catch every woman's eye,
isn't it?

and there's a dark side of me
that would elongate the pain
for justice.
she would suffer longer
just to hear the truth,
she'd find out the secrets
before hearing them from you.

and she's going to stay sweet
and not give you a reason
to avoid face to face communication
just so she can ask you who ria is.

i would have hated you by now
if i said i **loved** you and meant it,
but all of my 'i **love** you's' were just
something i said
for all the things that you did–
now all i feel is indifference.

you can think what you want

but don't think for a second
that it didn't hurt me,

don't think just because i'm strong
i can't feel a thing,

don't think that when you left
it changed everything

because while you may be gone,
nothing's changed,

and maybe that's the problem.

maybe I need a new place,
a new dress,
or a new hair color.

you took my name away from me—
turned it into something different entirely,
made me have to rethink myself—
reinvent myself
into someone you'll never get to know,
never get to touch.

for christmas,
i hope you get everything
you asked for.

when you decided to betray me.

do the walls in your condo remember me?
who else have they seen?
is there ever a time
they echo my name?
and is that sound deafening?

i think the loneliest feeling is
missing someone
and not being able to tell them
because that version of them
no longer exists.

i'm not leaving the person i knew
or the person i wanted you to become;
i'm leaving the person you were all along.

you can keep
your secrets,
but you can't
keep me.

it was wonderful playing
make believe with you,
but i'd like the real thing now.

it's sad, really,
because while you were the one
who lied to me the most,
you were the one
who treated me the best.

i don't regret you,
and if i had the chance
to take our time back,
i wouldn't.
i **loved** us
for all we were,
all we weren't,
and all we will never be,
even if it turned out
to be nothing but a lie–
a made-up bedtime story
you read to me,
and i listened to like a child,
smiling because i believed in every one.
you were a prince and i, your princess
until suddenly,
there were no pages left to turn.

"don't worry," i tell my mom
"he picks me up for date nights"
but so did you.

"don't worry,
he also supports me and calls me beautiful"
but so did you.

"i mean it, don't worry, mom
he supports my dreams and makes me better"
but so did you.

"don't worry so much,
he says he wants to get married and have kids"
but so did you.

so maybe my mom should worry
because there are other men out there like you.

the one that
self-sabotaged.

i lean in closer
as you tell me about your day,
your beautiful dark eyes
let me know all that they've seen.
my only hope is that one day
maybe i'll hear the stories
come from your lips.

you fell in love
with my
self-defense
mechanisms.

your kisses were magic,
i couldn't just kiss you once.

sometimes the devil
doesn't have a tail and horns,
sometimes he wears ray bans
and drives a range rover.

sometimes he doesn't appear evil–
he even cares about you a little,
and his smile makes you suspiciously happy
when maybe it should scare you.

sometimes the devil
isn't who you think he is
because he lies,
and sometimes he's lying in your bed.

you didn't give me nothing,
but you didn't give me everything.
you gave me just enough,
just enough
to keep me waiting,
just enough
to let me know we had something,
just enough
to give me hope it could be forever.

i fell in **love** with your chaos,
i fell in **love** with the not knowing,
with all your inconsistencies
keeping me on my knees,
begging you to stay or leave.
it was a fun little game
we kept playing,
it kept me waiting
for more
or for change.
you kept me on my toes,
and i let you
because i fell in **love** with our chaos,
i fell in **love** with the not knowing.

if i had a choice, i wouldn't forget you;
i'd just remember you like this:

i want to remember you sitting at dinis
next to your friend
for moral support,
that was the first time we met.
i want to remember how my heart dropped
seeing you in that floral button-down shirt.

i want to remember our walk on the beach that day,
and how you lifted me up on the boardwalk
just for us to get too hot a few minutes later.
i want to remember us guessing the costs
of dream houses we saw,
and how you'd win every time because
of your realtor experience,
or how i finally told you i had to pee
and you laughed and said thank God
because you had to too.

i want to remember you on our spontaneous trip
to san francisco–
we barely knew each other then
so things were still light and fun.

i want to remember how you kept looking
at me in awe,
and i'd ask "what?" as if something was wrong,
and you'd just smile and say i scared you.
and it wasn't because i was crazy
because i was not,
but there's times i think we could have fallen
in **love**.

i never knew what that meant,
and i guess i never had to
because our time came and went
a little too quick.

i want to remember you on that night
you moved to my city,
and i helped you carry bag after bag
to a 23rd floor–
downtown was crowded that night
because of bad bunny,
i want to remember all those awkward
elevator rides
because you didn't know how to talk to me,
yet somehow, you fascinated every fiber
in my being.

i want to remember all those nights
i was deep in anxiety
because of how much i was falling for you.
i want to remember the feeling all those things
i had only ever felt once before
and all those times you made me feel safe again
just talking with you.

i know i'll never forget you but there's some things
i want to forget.

i wish i didn't remember your trip to LA
and your agenda,
which was your first lie to me.
i wish i could forget the things i can't prove
but the things i know deep within me.

i wish i didn't remember that night you came back
from the east coast,
i wish i could forget you going
to your friend's birthday party
and picking me up drunk,
but sometimes i think i liked you better drunk;
that's when i got to know the truth.

i wish i didn't remember that phone call we had
when you were drunk at 1 AM
and demanded me in your bed.
i wish i could forget all the awful things you said.

i wish i didn't remember our last call
when you'd noticed i'd been distant.
i wish i could forget you telling me
to have a nice life
then hanging up in an instant.
after i finally learned to set boundaries,
i guess you decided you couldn't grow up.

maybe some day
i'll remember to forget you
or forget to remember you.

they ask me how i could miss you–
you're a liar,
you're a cheater,
you hurt me over and over,
but you weren't just a liar
or a cheater–
you were there for me
when no one else was,
you were there when i needed a hug,
you made me laugh
in moments i felt lost,
you fulfilled the adventure
i was yearning for,
you made me feel alive
when i was numb–
doesn't that count for something
even if it came at a cost?

thank you for what you did for me
and for what you didn't.

i'm not trying to
save you anymore,
i'm fine with
watching you
self-destuct.

sometimes i don't think it's you
that i miss
but the moments
i may never get again–
the memories that couldn't have a duplicate
with feelings that know all the places i've been.
they seem to hold the power
to make me push send
when i promised myself
i'd just let it end.

you want me crazy,
you want me out of my mind,
you want to take all that is mine–
so you can be my everything
you want me to say goodbye
to my self-esteem,
all my laughter, all my joy,
down to my personality–
so i can look at you as the one and only light
when we both know
it's been me this whole time.
you see me as something shiny,
but you're afraid i'll outshine you.
i want to shine together,
but all you know is power–
you could rule this world
but what does that mean, really,
if you don't have me?

you weren't mad at me,
and for some reason i wished you were.
at least then i'd know i still mattered,
and we'd still have something worth fighting for.

my heart has been broken before,
scattered in many pieces
and tossed all along the floor,
but no matter how much it hurt,
i always went back for more–
opening my heart up
for someone new;

that is,
until i met you.

you came to me
somewhere out of the blue
at a time when i was lost
and confused.

all you knew was small talk,
my soul yearned for depth.
all you knew was money,
my heart craved meaning.
all you knew was reputation,
my mind understood perception.

i knew from the beginning
you weren't mine,
you never were.

so why was it you?
why were you the last straw?

i knew you'd come back,
i knew you'd miss me eventually.
i knew there'd come a time
you couldn't drive fast enough
to out run my memory
or drink enough
to escape every thought of me.
all the girls you slept with
just weren't me.
all the time you spent with people
to run away from yourself and me
left you lonely?

call me crazy,
but if you have the opportunity
to go back to an ex,
i think it'd be wrong if you didn't.
if there's something there,
after years of growth,
you have something worth fighting for.

they say good
things don't last,
so let's just
be bad.

you just had your 30th birthday
and i'll be married soon.
no, i don't know to who,
but you're weighing heavy
on my mind tonight,
and i was just thinking–
maybe we should see each other
just one last time,
so we can laugh and joke
and be best friends again,
and i can ask you if you're still telling lies,
and you can smile and shake your head.
then i'd finally get to see the sorrow in your eyes
as you'd tell me
you're ready to find mrs. right,
and we can recall our past
without any resentment this time,
even if it's just for a couple hours,
even if it's to feel something or nothing
or just to feel like ourselves again.
maybe i hope you've changed,
or maybe i hope you haven't.

i couldn't care less
about the show we're watching,
but i could watch it forever
if it meant not ever having to leave
this moment with you.

DON'T YOU GET IT?
I ONLY HATED YOU
BECAUSE
I LOVED YOU!

you asked me what i'd do if the world was to end in 30 minutes. but i don't think you could handle what i'd say next. so i stayed quiet. but if i was to speak, i know i'd say this:

if the world was really ending in 30 minutes, i know i'd tell you i used to hate you. i'd make sure you understood that the opposite of **love** isn't hate, but indifference. and i hated you so much. but for the first time, i'd tell you i **love** you. i wouldn't need more time to try to decide. i'd **love** you without hesitation and without fear and without pride. because there's no longer a reason not to. after all, all our hardships would mean nothing in the next 30 minutes. there would be nothing left for us in this world other than **love**. and with the clock ticking, i'd remember all the things you've done for me and all the times you were there for me. i'd tell you how grateful i was for you. i'd tell you how amazing of a person you are. and how i'd hope we'd get to spend more time together in the next life. i'd tell you i **love** you because we don't have time for another fight or another betrayal. we don't have time to screw this up. there would finally be no time for anything else to get in the way of us. all we'd have time for is **love** and that's all i'd feel because nothing else would matter. i'd tell you i **love** you even if i didn't know it before the 30 minutes started. even if i was running from it. even if i was trying to fight it. i'd know it then. i'd say it. and we'd have to make **love** like we never have before and never will again. then i'd ask you to kiss me just one last time. and we'd go on to shoot one another at the same exact time to halt any unnecessary suffering. because i'd want to die in that moment. i'd want to die happy and with you. there would be nothing left to live for because we already lived everything we needed to.

we are the craziest
thing i've ever known.

i told you
i **loved** you that night
by accident.
it just came out of me
like a hello or a goodbye.
i didn't have a reason to **love** you,
in fact, i had every reason not to,
but this was the first time
i wasn't in transactional **love**.
i thought to myself:
what a beautiful thing
to **love** someone for the things
i cannot see.

you say you don't want
a woman who's crazy
until you meet one.
suddenly,
you become fascinated
and infatuated with her;
you fall for her insanity,
her unpredictability,
and all her chaos.
then you shake your head
and you call her crazy,
but what you don't tell her
is that you like it–
you like when she speaks her mind,
even when it challenges yours,
and how she can see the unseen,
and how she makes you feel alive–
even on a random tuesday.
sure, you've seen crazy before
the kind that slashes tires
and slams doors,
but the craziest woman
you've ever known
is the one who keeps you on your toes,
the one who made you fall in **love**,
even when you promised you never would.

there's a girl in orange county,
isn't there?
i don't know her name,
but i know you see her from time to time.
the effort you put into her
is something i wish was mine.

if the truth is
you have changed
like i always wanted you to,
and you've moved on
with someone new,
then leave me ignorant,
leave me delusional,
leave me happy,
just please,
don't leave me.

i hate falling for you
because i have to be

ready to leave at any
given time.

i smiled as i looked at you,
and a tear fell down my face
as i realized how much i **loved** you.
i **loved** you for everything you were
and for everything you weren't;
i **loved** you for all you did for me
and all the things you wouldn't;
i **loved** you for all the time we had spent
and all the time i wish we had left;
i **loved** you for the reasons we're together
and even the reasons we will never last.

and there we were
in every picture,
in every memory,
acting like
we had the rest of our lives to be together,
but knowing we didn't.

was it all fake?
was it all for show?
was it just a façade
to make me think
what i didn't already know?

i'm going to get married soon.
no, i don't know his name
or even where he stays,
but i know he wants me;
he makes it known,
he doesn't play mind games.
instead, he knows how to communicate,
and he's humbly successful,
he leads from his heart,
he's not only courageous in business,
but in romance as well–
but he's not crazy like you,
and he can't make me laugh like you do.

they'll never
be better than you,
but they'll be better
for me.

the one that
went ghost.

all the times you fake sleep
to avoid talking about feelings,
i know you're not actually asleep
until you moan.
i've never heard someone do that before,
but i like it
because you let me hear it,
and i like when you're asleep
because i know you struggle to fall asleep
like me.
that's something i **love** about you
and about us
because at every sleepover
when i was young
all the other girls used to fall asleep
before me,
and i felt so alone
somehow you make me feel less lonely.

i'm not a morning person
and i hate sleeping next to someone,
but i like when your alarm goes off
at six in the morning,
and you tell me i can go back to sleep,
but as you take your long shower,
i can't feel you next to me
and soon i just can't sleep,
so i get up
to spend more time with you
before you leave,
and i wish all my mornings
were like these.

in the morning
you go to your bathroom
and i go to mine.
you take a long shower,
and let thoughts of me dance in your mind,
while i stare out the kitchen window
replaying everything from last night.
then you walk out
and ask what i see outside.
i tell you:
a construction site
and crows flying by,
but we don't say much in the mornings
because we don't need to
or we don't know how to–
we just laugh and smile
in the awe that is today,
and i let you hug me
for a long time;
before i go
i ask for just one more,
and i think we've learned
that one more
is never enough.

i asked you
how you define **love**,
and you told me
you didn't know what that was.

i could wait my entire

life for you.

but i can't wait

for nothing.

i turned around
and said, "have an amazing day"
then i walked out the door.
there never was a goodbye
because i thought
i'd see you again soon.
if i had known that'd be the last time,
maybe i would have leaned into your hug
a little tighter and a little longer,
maybe i would have looked back at you
and memorized the lines on your face
in fear i'd someday forget,
but after a year
i still haven't.

you texted me merry christmas
and happy new year;
there was no
happy valentine's day,
st. patrick's day,
easter,
or cinco de mayo.

the goodbyes i hate the most
are the ones that never come.
instead, they get lost in final hugs
and last conversations.
before we know it,
we find ourselves leaving
with the hope of seeing each other again.
funny,
we think these moments
would always be planned.
i guess that's why it hurts so bad.

you're an amazing man;
you're just afraid of **love**,
and i can't blame you
because if you didn't run away,
i know i would have.

it shouldn't be hard–
living without you.
after all, i did it once before
except now-
now i know what i'm missing.

i miss your mystery–
how do you sleep at night?
on your stomach or on your back?
do you drink coffee in the morning?
and if so, do you like it black?
why are you so happy when you're with me,
but can't find the time to text me back?

i miss your mystery–
the times i wondered about
what i thought i could know.

sometimes there's a rhyme to your reason,
and sometimes there's no reason at all.

i miss the way your scent
used to linger on me for days,
a faint cologne mixed with weed and sage.

i miss the way your body felt
lying next to mine,
just your warm presence was enough,
but we cuddled half the time.

i miss the laughs we once shared
over knowing familiar unknown places
in different years
and the same faces.

i miss the way we used to argue
over meaningless shit.
my passion craved yours,
but we knew when to quit.

i miss the man
who held me close
to calm my anxiety.

i miss lying there in your arm,
my hand on your naked chest
as i felt your heartbeat,
you held and kissed my head.

its small moments like that
that i wonder if we'll ever get back.
i wasn't done with you yet;
are you never coming back?

i miss the way you lit up
when i entered the room.
i thought it would fade
after four junes.

i miss you
with every fiber in my being.
i hope you're going through it,
but i hope you're healing

because your actions
are out of character,
but the man you once were
can't be the man you are now.

i **loved** you then,
and i **love** you now.

our apartment 1412 days
have been lived,
now where have you gone?
is our time locked away
in that 2-bedroom home?

i know someone else lives there by now;
they're sleeping where we slept,
eating where we ate,
seeing what we saw,
but they don't know the history
behind those walls.

somewhere in the back of our minds
lies halloween on a monday night,
and the look in my eyes
when i took your hand
and walked you to your bathroom,
so, we could analyze our heights.
i laughed when you thought i was 5'5
because that's the shortest you'd date;
kinda like i'd only get twisted with you
with anyone else it just wouldn't feel right.

we are so different,
you and i,
but you never claimed to be,
and neither did i.
some things we never had to say
because words can't replace energy,
like i can't replace you,
and there's no replacement for me.

I read
somewhere on the internet
that sage repels spiders,
so every night
i burn the stick
you gave to me.
it's hard to believe
it's been over a year now,
and you've still found
a way to protect me.

i don't remember when i fell in **love** with you,
all i know is
it had been two months
since we talked,
and after a movie night
i told my best friend
that i just hoped you were alright,
even if we never do speak again,
and i never get to know the reason
because i **love** you anyway,
and those three words
came out on their own;
i couldn't hold them in,
and it stunned me into oblivion.

i rarely talk about you. i don't tell people you're the reason i moved to this city like i've always wanted to. or how a conversation with you inspired me to accomplish my childhood dream of finally becoming an author. no one knows how we would argue most of the time or how our disagreements never ended in bitterness but in more **love** and acceptance. and if today i was to say your name, everyone would know how tough you are, but no one would know all the stories you shared with me. you don't let people know your history. well, no one except me. i don't tell people that the last thing you ever said to me was "happy new year" once we finally got closer. but the people i talk to know me or see me as i am right now, and i can never be the woman i was before you. so in a way they already know you.

and as for everyone who knows about my days with you, they all think i don't talk about you because i'm over you. but really, i don't talk about you because i'm afraid you're the greatest **love** i'll ever have. the truth is, i'm terrified. i'm terrified that knowing you is the reason i picked this life. and if that's true, what does that leave for my future? i know i will find other **love** elsewhere. perhaps i'll even get married and have a family like i've always wanted. but what if that part of me is always waiting for you? even if i'm waiting for nothing.

you weren't the man i was looking for, but you were everything i ever needed. you aren't my greatest **love** because you were the perfect gentleman or treated me like a princess or could give me everything i ever wanted. you are my greatest love because you were my best friend and you understood things about me that no one else ever did. you are my greatest **love** because of the way we lit up when we were together. and the first time we met we knew we had already spent years together. you aren't my greatest **love** because we spent decades or long amounts of time together, you are my greatest **love** because you made three years feel like i could move on to the next life. we spend our lives trying to define and organize **love** but our greatest **love** often doesn't make sense.

i have been **loved** by many men,
and i have **loved** many men
in my life
all the same, yet so differently,
but i couldn't bring myself to stay with any,
and i met you somewhere in the middle of all
of them.
you seem to have something they don't,
you're just worth it in the end.
through every argument and every fight,
i can still feel my **love** for you,
and yearn to be with you every night.

i fell in **love** with you as you fell in **love** with her. i watched as she changed parts of you. she was so needy so you had to see her daily. tell me, were you using her or was it the other way around? but no matter how toxic she was for you, you couldn't get enough of her. you became an addict. i always wondered what she had that i lacked. but i fell out of **love** with you as you fell down for her bad. tell maryjane i said hi.

i used to hate how you smoked so much.
i always used to think
it clouded your judgment,
but these days i buy weed.
just to smell it,
and i get high
when i think of the time
you had me roll it.
honestly,
i don't even like weed,
but because of you,
there's a part of me
that **loves** it.

there's a truck parked
outside this coffee shop
that looks like yours,
and i've began to wonder
what i'd do if it was.

all the hours i've spent
in anger and sadness,
but i still think if i saw you now
my soul would light up,
and i'd run up
to hug you
like nothing ever happened.

and that scares me a little
to know that i'm capable
of doing something
so far from my intention.

i still hear your voice saying
certain things; it's funny,
really, because i haven't
heard it in years.

all the things we've said,
and all the things we left unsaid–
they're floating in a different reality,
and i can't help but wonder
if we're together there.

i thought i was obsessed with you. after all, i had nothing left to do but think of you since i couldn't see you. and i liked that. in fact, i craved that time i had to think you into the man i'd like you to be for me. you stayed away from me so i didn't have to know the man you are. somehow i knew you always wanted to protect me. but what we had was never **love**. what we had was distance. nothing more, nothing less. and i'm afraid i've fallen in **love** with being alone instead, something far worse than being in **love** with someone who can't commit.

i used to cry over your silent goodbye,
i used to believe every one of your lies,
i used to spend far too long wondering why,
i used to wait and wait for a reply.

but now
all i have is thank you's–
thank you for leaving and taking all
the poison with you,
thank you for hurting me so deeply
i'd have no other choice but to stop seeing people
like you,
thank you for leaving me
so i could believe in **love** and men again,
thank you for never switching up;
making me realize what signs
i missed from the jump,
thank you for treating me like shit
so i can start asking myself
what i need and deserve,
thank you for leaving my life
so i could finally make room for a man of his word.

i don't want your breadcrumbs, baby;
i want the whole loaf.
i want the focaccia, sourdough,
and all the scones–
i need the damn bakery.

i'm scared that i've met my person
but that person isn't the one i'll marry,
and that's a strange problem to have.

he sat across from me:
two glasses of wine,
dim candle light,
"have you ever been in **love**?"
i heard him ask.
as he looked me in the eye,
i smiled and looked down–
visions of you and us danced in my mind,
but i looked up from my wine
and replied,
"i don't recall a time."

i met someone.
he treats me so well,
he really does,
and he wants to marry me.
he knew that after the fourth date.
you don't believe in marriage
and you never will,
but you know i do,
and i'm not here to change your mind
i'm just here to say goodbye.

a year ago
if you told me,
once i let that man go,
i could have everything i've ever wanted,
my world would feel like magic
and living would be the easiest thing
i'd ever do.
opportunities would come to me
like a missing puzzle piece,
and i'd meet a man
like the one i write about in every journal entry
one that knows **love**,
and who's not only good
but who's good for me.
i would have told you
i didn't want it;
i'd rather have him
or really the idea of him.
i'd choose to just sit there
and wait to live
or wait to die,
and now i realize that man took my life–
not because he's a killer,
not because he's a bad man,
but because i was the one with the knife,
stabbing myself in the back several times,
telling myself i didn't need to live;

i just needed him,
and it scares me
to think if i got everything i ever wanted then,
i wouldn't know what it feels like to live.

the one that

moved away,

i told you that my greatest fear
was marrying someone
who didn't genuinely **love** me,
and you said,
"that could never happen"
but i guess my real fear is
marrying someone who i don't truly **love**.
i've known so many different **loves**–
how will i know when one is worth it?

if you knew me in my weaker moments,
would you still **love** me?
i've been strong all my life,
but i want to weep in your arms–
i want to fall apart,
and i want you to catch me.
i want to expose all my imperfections
just to see you still there next to me,
and while my world falls apart,
i want to die in your arms
without you trying to rescue me.

i like the way you say my name. and trust me when i say i don't mean that in a sexual way. you don't know this, but there was a time before you i started to hate it. like i never thought i could. i had always been so proud of it until people ruined it. i like the way you say my name. in consideration, compassion, and intention. my name means something to you. it feels safe upon your lips. reborn again. rejuvenated.

it's beautiful when
they'd lie for you,
but it's a red flag too.

i fell in **love** with the 2015 twitter version of you i wasn't supposed to meet. i guess i'm one of the few to find **love** while stalking instead of heartbreak. at first, i never thought we had anything in common. i guess you ran away because i reminded you of the person you used to be. before all the corruption, money, lies, and drug addiction.

i knew you long enough
to miss you,
but i miss you
because i didn't know you long enough.

i can't help but wonder
what my life would be like
if i would have went away with you–
packed up everything
and chose **love** this time.

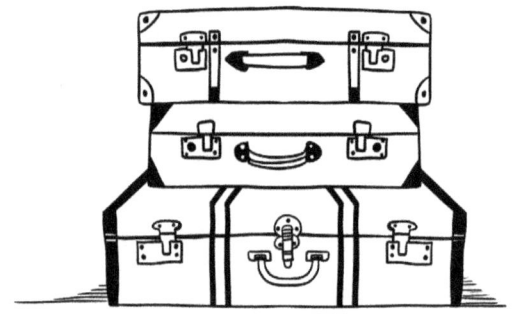

you want to pretend like you don't care.
i get it, i do.

you want me to write about you,
you want me to tell of all the feelings
we don't speak about.
you want me to write
about our **love's** vacancy–
all the things that were
and all the things that could be,
but you're all
i've ever written about.
you're the stars, the moon,
the **love**, the pain;
you're everything
i've ever felt.

i hate how happy i am
that you're back in town
because it broke my heart
when you left.

my door will always be open for you to leave. to run away. to abandon all responsibility. you're not my hostage. although sometimes i just wish you'd choose to stay. if i had it my way, you'd choose me over all your fears.

baby, you're not consistent. don't lie to yourself or to me. let's not trick ourselves even for a second into believing there's something more than what we've got. we know there's no stability here. there's no future waiting for us. years ago i would have liked that. you know i'd be begging you to change and sacrificing myself in the process. but i've learned how to **love** unconditionally now. i've learned how to say i **love** you for who you are even if that person is a nomad. a man on the run. a man who can't commit or just won't. i've learned how to be okay with that. now i know how to say i **love** you, but i don't want you back.

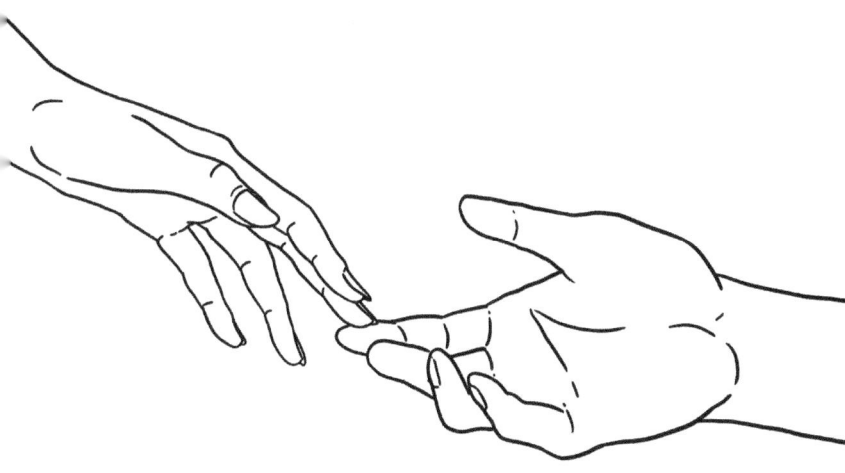

the one that

let me go,

you get me in ways i hoped no one ever would.
you're the safest and most dangerous paradise
i've ever known. for that reason, i hate knowing
you because i'm haunted by the fear of one day
not being able to.

your silence is mysterious
like the one color in your eyes
when you look at me
as i tell you things i don't usually say,
fading into speechlessness
after the depths of my soul are exposed,
and you haven't run away.

the world sees me as a light,
but only you see the darkness
that makes me shine so bright.

i like the way you undress me
without using your hands,
pulling back layer after layer
using only questions and eye contact.
then you stay and watch,
what a seductive act.
and after you get me naked,
you go deeper than i've ever had;
feeling every part of me,
and we haven't even gotten to the climax.
i like when you're inside me;
we don't just have sex.

i like seeing you naked
with all your clothes on.

i tell you things
i don't want to tell you.
you make me feel too safe;
it's dangerous.

you left me because you know i want **love**,
but i don't want to be stuck.

you **love** every part of me
with acceptance and patience,
you know the parts of me
that quiver under commitment,
you **love** the parts of me
that aren't relationship worthy.
you don't try to change me;
you just **love** me,
even if we're miles apart,
and you found another girl
to keep you warm
while i'm away
breaking your heart.

five years
turned into one final night.
we had five goodbyes
when we didn't even want to have one.

do you think i could get a hug for the road?
could you wrap up the feeling
of your arms wrapped around me
and i'll take it to go?
i'll save it for a day
that will never come
because i never want you to hug me
for the last time.
i never want to know
what that feels like.

i knew you weren't
the one, i just didn't think
the end would ever come.

cognitive dissonance;
tell me
we won't see each other again,
then pull me in close
and kiss my forehead.

you told me i won
because i had your mind,
but maybe i lost
because i wasn't the one
lying by you every night.

we said goodbye,
but something
told me it wasn't
the end.

you kissed her today
with the lips you kissed me with last night,
why?

i could ruin your relationship with her
if i wanted to,
but i don't
because the **love** you have with her
makes sense
like yours and mine never will.

there was **love** there,
just not the **love** that lives together
and has a family
and says "i do" to forever,
but there was **love** there—
so much **love**.

no one

in particular,

you called me beautiful
then sat down to eat your taco.
i smiled as i explained
that if that's all i was to you
this just wasn't going to work.
i don't want to live that narrative
where two beautiful people
get married and move to the suburbs,
have two kids and a white picket fence,
but the husband cheats
and the wife's on antidepressants.
where they appear to have it all
but really have nothing
because they live in a home with no **love**.
i told you
i want to be cared for when i'm sick,
and i want support while giving birth to your kids,
and i want to be looked at the same way
at 83 as i was at 23.
i want to be beautiful,
but i don't want to be JUST beautiful.
you looked up from your margarita,
smiled, and said, "that's a relief".

after this kiss
and after this sunset,
no matter how today ends,
even if you leave
or i die
or we never speak again,
you reminded me that i can **love**
and how great that is.

i want a hug from you,
i want a conversation,
i want to know where you've been
before this moment we're sharing,
and what you're doing now.
i want to know what you're passionate about,
tell me the times you wanted it all to end
and what kept you going.
i want to know what keeps you awake at night,
and the last time you felt lonely
and while you're at it,
tell me why i'm drawn to you
without even knowing you.

i messed things up with you.
you're a nice guy,
so you never told me i did.
i guess
i'm just afraid i'll do it again.

you look like my past. an exciting and chaotic time, i might add. sometimes i miss it. i even yearn for it on occasion. i find myself envying that version of me who didn't have to think before doing things. the spontaneity. the freedom. all the fun i had. how i got lost in every moment. i didn't need to live by a plan. but it wasn't good for me then. and it certainly isn't good for me now. so don't look at me like that. don't say what you're about to say before you kiss me. because i'm afraid once you do, there's no going back. and i can't go back. i can't be the girl i used to be. i've seen too many things and learned too many lessons. i spent time that i can't get back. and all it did was just leave me empty handed. i can't repeat that pattern with you no matter how badly i want to.

you remind me of someone,
someone that i **love**.
and i feel like
i'm already wasting your time
because when i look at you,
i see him.

i said my last goodbye to you today,
but i know it's not the end.
i know i'll see you somewhere else again.
it may be
days,
weeks,
months,
years,
or another lifetime.

my eyes are staring at
the wall in front of me,
but all i can see

is your memory.

i miss you in a way
that doesn't know what's missing.
i lay awake at night,
caressing a pillow trying to remember
what it felt like
to touch you,
to hug you,
to be with you,
to call you mine.
i contemplate what it means
to remember you
without remembering you.
i know there was a time
i used to know all the lines on your face
down to your nose's shape.
i used to know the password to your phone
and what time you'd usually be home
to how you fall asleep at night.
i wonder if i still know you.
now, i just think i know that i miss you
for what i can and cannot remember,
for the parts of you that were me
or suddenly became me.
do i miss you?
or do i just miss not being lonely?

what is time?
if nothing else
other than what's keeping us apart?
all i know is a time with you,
and a time after you–
you're how i tell time,
you're how i know sorrow.
nothing else seems to matter
as nothing changes,
even when everything does.
i'm destined to know a future of
wrinkle after wrinkle,
gray hair after gray hair,
holiday after holiday,
year after year.
and i'm still here while i'm there,
telling you things i never told my family,
laughing when you do- well anything,
being more than happy to do nothing
because being with you
gave my life meaning.

i'm craving change,
any kind of change,
and all change.
i just can't be the woman
who **loved** you anymore
because that woman's heartbroken.
she can't move right now,
she can't think,
she can barely breathe,
i can't be her,
i have to keep moving.
it's not an identity crisis
if you can't identify with it.

i'll never steal your phone. but if i did, i wouldn't look to see who you're following or who you're texting. instead i'd go to your notes app. i'd like to know what's on your mind, what keeps you up at night, what's on your grocery list, and what things you don't want to forget. maybe then i'd be able to decide if it's you i like, or steve or mike instead.

you cannot break me.
i grew up with a broken heart;
it feels like home to me.

i grew up where **love** was loud–
it was yelling and breaking dishes,
it was disputes and living in tension,
it was competition and secrecy.
who could **love** who louder?
it was power and control and walking on eggshells,
it was fighting to stay together
because you **loved** the chaos
more than each other.
i learned passion and possessiveness,
i witnessed cheating and resentment,
i watched the focus be on appearance
rather than how it felt within,
but that **love** was all i've ever known.

so yes,
our silences scared me,
our conversations were alarming,
your patience was a mind game.
every good thing was one shoe
waiting for the other one to drop.
our time apart told me you didn't **love** me,
and when you ended it to let me be myself,
in my mind,

you didn't want to fight for us.

i never knew how unconditional **love** felt.

it was hard for me to hear the whisper of your **love**

because all i've ever known was a **love** that's loud.

if you're going to **love** me,
don't **love** me halfheartedly.
don't say i **love** you
while looking at my beauty
but not seeing through me.
don't **love** me for one part of me
while trying to change another.
don't **love** me for what we could be,
instead, accept me for me,
and if you can't **love** me fully,
then don't love me at all.

don't **love** me because you think i'm perfect,
love me instead
because you know not to talk to me
before i've had my morning coffee
or because you know to tell me to be ready at 8
so i'm actually ready by 8:30.
tell me you **love** me despite
all my sensitivity and curb checking
or for my long night routine
or how i always have to get up to go pee.
tell me you know all those things about me
and you **love** me anyway.

.

"the one,"

the one that you're looking for doesn't exist. i don't say this with anger, bitterness, jealousy, or regret. i say this as an unidentified realist. the idea of the one is only meant to keep you away from **love**.

love will not save you–
instead, it will show you all the things
you've been running from.
it will cost you all your selfishness, pride,
and patience.
it will highlight all the things about yourself
that you don't like,
it will tear you up inside
and corner you into feeling everything,
facing everything.
it will leave you so exposed
that you'll want to run and hide,
but it will be the best thing
that's ever happened to you
all at the same time.

i don't think **love** is what they tell us it is. i don't think **love** is what we want it to be either. contrary to what most people believe, i don't think **love** ever goes away. in a world where everything is temporary, our jobs, our homes, the money in our bank account, our feelings, or even life itself- **love** is the only thing that lasts. it's the most divine encounter we can ever have, but sometimes it comes at a cost.

this world will tell you to get married for the rest of your life, and if it ends in divorce there's no **love** left. this world will tell you that if that person leaves, there's no **love** left. this world will tell you that if a friendship ends, there was no **love** to begin with. while the world paints in black and white, **love** is color. **love** can't be easily defined.

i'm avoiding dating, and i think it's because i'm afraid i'll eventually find a good man. someone supportive. someone with morals and reason. someone i could build a life with. and i guess i'm unsure of what to do with my thoughts of you. will they just vanish? everyone says they will, but i'm afraid they're all liars. how can i marry another man when you have my head?

i've never told
anyone this,
but i'm afraid.
i'm afraid that all
i've ever wanted
is a lie.

i always wonder
if the people who get married
are happy and actually want to,
or if, deep down, there's a part of them
that cries not to.
i wonder if there is a kind of **love** out there
strong enough to silence
all cries for freedom.

i think what i fear most
is telling my grown child
about the one i **loved**
who isn't their father.

you're a good man,
just not my man–
but how i wish you could be
because if you're not,
then i have to get back out on these streets.

my darling,
everyone you **love** will leave you,
in matters of choice, betrayal, or death,
and everyone you're close to
will hurt you.
you just have to decide
if that **love** is worth it in the end.
sometimes **love** isn't enough,
but sometimes it is.

i give you permission to **love**
like you've never been hurt,
know that it's safe to
because every heart break
that you've been through
you've gotten through.
each one showed you
a part of yourself
you hadn't met yet.

i think that we could have spent our lives with multiple people. i believe that the people who once broke our hearts are still our soul mates. because behind every hurtful event or off timing, there was a connection there. i don't think you should feel like you have to stop loving them. just **love** them from a distance. **love** them despite the hurt they caused you. let that **love** consume you. find it in every person you've met. i don't think soul mates are one person but multiple people you have met whose souls you connected with. i think you chose one soul mate to live your life with based on timing and behavior. but that doesn't make the ones before them any less of a soul mate, so **love** them from a distance. let that **love** consume you because it's only the hate, anger, and guilt you have for still loving them that stops you from letting yourself **love** and be **loved** fully. so let yourself **love** them. **love** them from a distance with the knowledge that that's all you were meant to be: two people who were supposed to connect for a certain amount of time but ultimately are better off loving them from a distance. know there is someone who will suit you better in the long run. **love** is liberating.

anyone
reading
this,

sometimes i wish
a relationship was something
i could find at a grocery store
with an expiration date on it.
will it expire before it's all gone
is what i'd want to know.
however, if i were to see that date
i couldn't enjoy it,
but then again,
i don't choose food by the date.
i eat it until one random day
it doesn't taste the same.

maybe you can **love** someone
before you lose them,
but i think we never **love** someone more
than when we lose them.

i think what scares me
is that, at the end of the day,
there are no bad guys;
everyone's sane in their own mind.

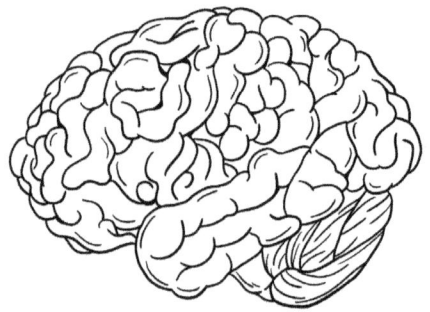

sex can't make them stay–
it might make them lie,
it might make them cheat,
but it can't make them stay.

in truth,
i don't think we say
"fuck you" to people
because they hurt us.
instead,
i think we say
"fuck you" to people
because they once cared–
they once gave us reasons
to trust them,
to let our guards down,
to find safety in them.

give me a second,
let me ask
my intuition.

the truth is
it's harder to admit you lost a good man;
it's much easier
to demonize them.

some nights i need hennessey
and others i just need poetry.

they ask me if i'm okay,
and i wonder what would happen
if i was to say i wasn't?
what could they say then
to help me, if anything
i'd get nothing,
so i lie
and tell them i'm okay.

one minute
we're living it
and the next
we're grieving it.

i can't quick-fix this.

there's certain videos in my phone
i can't watch anymore.
maybe because
i'm afraid i'll feel too much
or nothing at all.

clean sheets and shaven legs,
a movie on a friday night–
one to make me laugh
or one to make me cry
or maybe both.
just anything
to help me forget
how quiet it is in the city tonight.

no one tells you
how hard it is
to forgive yourself.

don't worry about me,
everything happens in my favor.

i have seen heartbreak
ruin people's lives,
sending them into dark depressions,
and i can't help but wonder
what's wrong with me?
why does it always feel good
being broken?

i've had my heart broken
several times before
by friends,
by **lovers**,
by backstabbers,
by cheaters,
but you saying
you don't know
what i should look for in a man
is the biggest heartbreak i've ever known.

my parents divorced when i was 16,
and since then,
i've made a promise to myself
i wouldn't be the same.
i thought if i studied every relationship book
and healed every part of my past
that needed healing,
i wouldn't crave heated arguments
and hot makeup sex.
i thought maybe then
i wouldn't want to be in a man's presence
who made me feel safe while feeling anxious.
i thought if i knew the difference
between **love** and attachment,
i would choose **love** without any hesitation.

i don't come from
a family where love
works out.

what do i want from **love**?
i used to be so sure.

i just logged back onto bumble,
and i see all but three
deleted accounts in my history.
i can't help but wonder–
have they all found **love**?
and am i the only one
who hasn't found someone?

i always say "see you" before leaving.
i don't even say "i'll see you" anymore
because maybe i won't.
i wonder how many people
had to leave my life
before i stopped saying goodbye?
i wonder how many hugs were the last time
or how many ex's and hoes
sent x's and o's
before going ghost?
i'm begging you to change my mind
as i write this with some hope,
but deep down, i know
if you **love** someone,
it's only a matter of time
before they go,
but i've learned that,
luckily, the **love** never leaves;
it just gets renamed to grief.

what if it's not sad
that thing you're going through
a death,
a breakup,
a loss of some kind?
what if it's not sad
because it means you're alive?

forever is a long time,
but with each year,
it gets a little closer to me.

all our problems in **love**
would dissipate
if we knew tomorrow
would never come.

www.ingramcontent.com/pod-product-compliance
Lightning Source LLC
Chambersburg PA
CBHW071727120626
46550CB00002B/418